Mouth Brimming Over

poems

Mouth Brimming Over

poems

by Roy Beckemeyer

BLUE
CEDAR
PRESS

Blue Cedar Press
PO Box 48715
Wichita, KS 67201

First edition
10 9 8 7 6 5 4 3 2 1

ISBN: 978-0-9960970-9-3

Cover photograph (Red-winged Blackbird at Quivira National
Wildlife Refuge, Stafford County, Kansas) and frontispiece image:
Copyright © 2019 by Roy Beckemeyer.

Author photograph (p. 119 and back cover): Courtesy of Jameson
Bayles.

Composition: Roy Beckemeyer
Cover Design: Roy Beckemeyer

"…a poem demands pronunciation. Poetry always remembers that it was an oral art before it was a written art. It remembers that it was first song."

— Jorge Luis Borges

Also by Roy Beckemeyer:

Stage Whispers
Amanuensis Angel
Music I Once Could Dance To

for two women I love:
my wife Pat and daughter Lori,
each a strong, caring, and brilliant individual

Contents

6   mouth brimming over / 97

1

fanfaronade

fanfaronade—a grandiose trumpet blast

With Apologies to Walt

I sing the body hydraulic. I sing the salted tears,
the plasma, the swollen hoses of veins and arteries,
the acrid urine, the flush of sweat pumped by fear,
the sheets of synovial fluid cushioning cartilage.

I sing bone-bound columns of spinal fluid washing silken
bundles of nerves. I sing the exudate and transudate,
the rheum, the chyle, serum and semen, the breast milk,
the bile, the amniotic fluid, the aqueous humor of sight.

I sing the body drenched, viscid, dripping, dewy.
I sing the body slippery, saturated, soggy.
I sing the body watery, liquid, clammy, fluid.
I sing the body succulent, sopped, sultry, sodden.

I sing ancient oceans where our antecedents frolicked.
I sing the body luscious. I sing the body hydraulic.

Singing to Myself

I will chime apocrypha
in bell-like plainchant,
never giving a glimmer,
a glimpse of how
I arrived at such
a notion of notes,
the words
tolling

in procession

like

monks

walking

kaihōgyō.

Red Tide

"The tulips should be behind bars like dangerous animals"
—Sylvia Plath

Red tulips roar at spring's otherwise pastel
and well-mannered new growth, rear
their heads and open their mouths wide
with the hunger of bulbs buried too long
in winter's grasp.

Their blood-drop shapes, the only heat
in spring's chill, encapsulate passion,
enflame youthful imagery. Girls slick
tulip's scarlet onto lips, boys lick their lips
for want of that color, hormones surge
and rush onto the shores of April, all
its barriers breached by a red tide
of tulips.

Ways of Flying

Swallows swirling seem to be
tugging at the selvage of the air's
very fabric, twisting loose threads
this way and that, sewing them back
in loops and twirls into the blue
shawl of day.

Vultures turn in slow, stately circles,
climb the oiled screw threads
of thermals, use the mechanical
advantage of the simplest machine
of air—the inclined plane—invisible
spiral pathway to the dizzying heights
of a summer day.

Coots scrabble at the trailing tails
of air kites, splash them with water,
make them visible with water drops
and froth, before finally grabbing hold,
lifting as if they were being pulled
by diamond-shaped darts on strings.

Cathedral

The architect pictures it rising abruptly—
a humpback whale broaching rolling Pacific
waves—a nascent volcano built upon
the molten basalt of Old Testament prophets—

"It should be iconic, come with cornices,
ionic columns, enfilades," he says. "It should
buttress our beliefs, accept the blue tint
of any one of a thousand days seen
from balustrades, porticos, mansard roofs."

"I will bind up board and batten, link loggia
with lintel, match and mix dormers, pilasters,
sacristies and fenestrations with love, with faith."

"I will arch my arms, outline bold basilicas,
monoliths to monotheism, let in the light
through clerestory, vault, transom—slit
the light with mullions, facet it with muntins."

"I will become arcuate, volute, pendentive.
I will draw with try-square, with compass;
ink onto vellum saintly names: Narthex.
Chancel. Nave."

"I will lift to luminance, with corbeled gestures
and archivolt soaring, every man's, every child's,
every woman's soul."

The old man's failing memory

squanders days the way water
spills over a river's dam—
extravagantly and with
the thrumming violence
of deep plunging, yet
catches glimpses of certain ones:
the silvery, salmon-shaped
twenty-four-hour-spans
that dart through the foam
of drenched decades to hover
within the brief glance
of his recollection. These
he secretes into the eddying
pool of remembrances where they
surface, sink, surface again,
play in alternating light
and shadow, translucent
green shallows, chocolate
brown depths, glint metal bright
or blood smeared carnelian,
the promise of dawn, the certainty
of dusk splashed along the bellying
tautness of sleek-torpedo bodies
and coin bright scales:
the blood-diamond currency
of the shrinking realm
of an aging mind.

Hail, *Amphibia*!

"…the hail, pea-sized, / froghops on the lawn"—
Kevin Rabas, "Hail"

Hail accretes itself in wild
roller-coaster rides we can only
experience in our dreams. Thrust
upward by express-elevator drafts,
tossed out on its own recognizance,
it soon violates its parole, falls in loop-
de-loop cycles, melts and freezes,
undergoes plastic surgery ignominies,
becomes lumpen, gargoyle-headed,
toad-warted, sort of round, layered
like an onion, but hard and brittle,
some layers translucent, others opaque,
one nearly transparent. It streaks
downward, heavy enough at last,
heft enough around its girth, to fall
like Newton's apple, to wedge itself
into sodden earth, crack and splinter
against concrete, bruise or shatter leaves,
conk branches, commit murder
on small birds, fracture cold-brittled
shingles, bounce off boards, jump,
like Calaveras County's favorite frog,
into the stream of lesser hailstones,
going the wrong way again, defying
for one last time the inevitability
of gravity's one-way street.

Gravestones and Bones

Long bones and short,
the bow-spring ribs,
the phalanges intricate,
the hollow thin eggshell-
skulls, the ball and socket
functionality, the pelvic
girdle through which
we all pass to life, soaked
and washed with blood
and flushed with the water
of cells, the fluid that bathes,
brings nourishment, and,
in turn, the aging and
wearing and breaking down,
to leave behind bones bare
as stones.

The slow lick of fluid the world
flicks at stone, the storm runoff,
the condensation, the fog,
the acid rain that wreak their work
in infinitesimal scales of dissolution,
the cycle of freeze and thaw
over a million seasons, the castle
walls inscribed with lichen and moss
that love moist granularity, wet
crevices, all the vastness of the world's
varied fastnesses crumbling
in their own sweet time.

Mephitis mephitis

The skunk takes up residence
beneath the deck, silky pelt,
moon-blast of white
ghosting across midnight-dark
urban grass, buoyant bearer
of that sweet musk the dog loves
in glancing measures, but recoils from
when, misinterpreting the front-
legged stance, the Mata-Hari dance,
the steamy embrace erupts
in her once inquisitive face.

Fire and Water

Fish as one with fluid flutter,
silver-green glimmers,
owe water no tribute,
druid-like in that sense,
immerse themselves
in becoming as watery
in their own way as how
the current flows, alter
the shallows with eddies,
bulldoze depths, sift silt
to mark with contrails
flips of fins, tails, filter,
with gills' carmine pleats,
the air there entrained,
to fan their flickering
metabolic flames.

Declension

Poison Ivy, *Toxicodendron radicans,*
pops up unwarranted, unwanted,

at random places around the garden,
marks where a robin hopped,

cocked its head, shot a white
stream, fecund lime, fecal streak,

where another rocketed into the air, splat
a whitewash surprise back at the resident cat,

a third tugged at a water-logged earthworm,
would have been grunting with effort if not

for its high-pitched syrinx, instead squirted
wet chalk and seeds into the grass.

Johnny-Ivy-Seed, Robin
Red-Rash, *Turdus migratorius*—

feathered practitioner of plant husbandry
[why never plant wifery?]—

agricola, agricolae,
agricolorum.

Conch Shells as Conveyances

"Mere air, these words, but delicious to hear."
—Sappho

Appetizer whispers
whet your wish for more.
Your seashell ears
long to nuzzle conch,
to close the feedback circuit
between ocean and air,
to lure out murmurs:
lush, smooth pink organic
shapes that bound
the infinitesimal space
between reverberations,
vertebrate to invertebrate,
cartilage curl to calcium
whorl, columellar fold
to cymbal curvature,
words-real or words-white-
noise, words whisked
from the world-without,
words born of spiraled
womb gone to nest in coiled
chamber, words smooth
as custard, ovoid as quail's eggs,
whipped cream words comprised
of the merest wisps of air.

Death's Gait

Neruda said that death's "steps can be heard
and its clothing makes a hushed sound, like a tree."
I wonder if its steps falter, like mine,
or if it treads confidently, its blind march
never involving a misstep, a stumble.
Perhaps Death, then, is a woodsman
who walks first-growth forests,
but who never steps on a twig,
a dead leaf, whose sleeve brushes
his waistcoat like leaves rustling in
the absence of breeze, whose trouser legs
have wide cuffs filled with the debris
of dead souls that rattles like seeds
missing from a dry gourd, whose slippers
grasp the sticky bit of nettle, drag it
over the flotsam of forest decay
with the sound of a bear rubbing
its flank against bark, walking its
flat-footed gait with the distinct
pattern of brain cells withering
in a cascading crescendo
of senescence.

The quote is from "Solo la muerte" ["Nothing but Death,"
translated by Robert Bly]

Falliteration

"...from the swells
they pulled flopping rainbows,"
he writes, fingering his pen,
flicking ash from his fag,
feeling every bit the western
scribe. We imagine him
as John Ford stereotype,
beefcake bard, powerful
poet, we think of versified
f-bombs, cowboy fables, falconers
on horseback, farriers, a farrago
of images, far-fetched, frantic,
all brought on by that foaming
flood below the falls.

The quote is from Greg Keeler's poem, "American Falls"

Celebration

You must hum your own lithe youth,
sing your exuberant childhood, raise
high the roof beams of coming of age,
shout the jubilation of adulthood.

Celebrating the exigencies of growing old,
you should trumpet the coup of you—ancient,
drone the dirge of you—dying. Then beam
the symphonic, operatic strains of you,
God's angel at last, flying.

Ikthýs

The white flesh of fish flayed
from silver-scaled armor's glisten:
the streamlined shape splayed
against blood-slimed wood. Listen

for the sound of a slender knife slicing,
the exhalation of swim bladder groan.
Philosophically enticing, this thought
of how the creatures we call food moan,

unheard, or at least unnoticed.
Oh, the chorus—when fishes and loaves
were prepared, the day when Jesus hosted
five thousand followers who roved

with Him the shores of Galilee;
did any hear the two fishes, cloven
over and over, by His hand, but He?
—those laments of fish, and men, interwoven.

Inspired by the poetry of Michael Cissell.

2

auricle

auricle—the mostly cartilaginous portion of the external ear; an atrium of the heart

Fifty-Eighth Anniversary

"their love is a slow tango"
—Traci K. Smith, "Astral"

Our love out-dances—
its choreography fleet—
the arthritic artifice
of our slow old feet.

Behold, the osteology
of ancient amour—
this terse tetralogy
of terpsichore:

Trendelenberg gait,
senescent shuffle,
the hitch upon rising,
the stumbling kerfuffle.

Totter's our two-step,
dotter our dance,
but our true *pas de deux*
is this fine-aged romance.

Artifact

If you were gone, I would be brittle ice, a
thin globe of glass surrounding filaments
incandescent, aging bone absent calcium, a
mere artifact you had dipped into liquid
nitrogen and struck, your arm swinging
back and high above your head: the sudden
hammer blow of your leaving.

Your cough

is the wracking avalanche
of flu turning virulent,
and I can feel the spraining
of your ribs that grate
beneath the bruise-blue
of weary muscles,
the thoracic girdle strained,
the helpless loss of control
of even the simple basic
expedient of breathing,
and my right hand, gentle
on your spasming back,
my left reaching for the box
of tissues, is such an inadequate
measure of my concern
that your thin *thanks*,
almost lost in the detritus
of loosening phlegm and gusting
plosives, is like an island
in these hurricane sneezes.

Topology

My shirt slips off
my shoulders (or your
skirt slides past your
hips), drops to the floor,
becomes a landscape
folded upon itself
(something it never
imagined when
carefully lain,
cleverly arranged
upon the closet shelf),
curves around
its own empty space
as if its memory
of the body's boundaries
has suddenly been
erased.

Spring Floods

All our rivers,
arteries of this land,
have burst like
aneurisms, bled out
clotted brown
across the green
skin of spring,
brought us all
to the point
of choking
on our own
life's blood.

Silos

Round for a reason,
standing tall,
silos watch over
what farmers do.

Filled full of silage,
they sigh at the lull
between seasons,
wrap around what

rapt field hands cut,
rake, auger. They wish
to last, to never lean,
to never shed shingle

or lath, never give up
guarding fields, lanes,
abandoned wheel-less
trucks, white-washed

farmsteads. They watch
over red barns, tousle-
headed kids, clucking chickens.
Rural mail carriers pull up

out front, their drive from
farm to farm punctuated
by silos, like pins stuck onto
the map of rural townships,

telling all who drive dusty
gravel roads there is life,
there are people, here,
right here, just below.

Kick

We have all half awakened
from that fluid slumber
of wetness, stirred in wombs,
flexed ourselves there
and quickened our mothers'
thoughts, wakened their fears,
raised up in them the emotions
mothers feel, waves of it
swelling arteries, generating
placental caresses,

      kick
              contract
     kick
              contract,

the tactile language
of the first and common chapter
of everyone's story.

Grieving

Grief shared remains
grief solely experienced
despite held hands,
grasping embraces, sobs
alternately wracking adjacent
shoulders, the rock-wall fits
of your head nestled against
my neck, my neck enfolding
crown of your head, the seed-
pearl tears of graded sizes
rifting identical ecosystems
of the rolling terrain of cheek
and chin, despite shared swims
in the roiling seas of grief,
paired tumbles from cliffs
tall as decades of love
and cohabitation, despite
the mirrored infinities
of the cavernous emptiness
of my eyes as reflected back
from yours.

Emigrants, 1857

The sea, strange and cold
to landsmen, seems to pierce
the hull of steerage holds
where gray and brown clad
children, mothers, huddle there,
the fields around Minden still
bright in the hippocampus depths
of their minds, and in the roll
and pitch of seas they perhaps
recall the wagon ride to church
on winter's rutted roads and,
in their sturdy Lutheran way,
they kneel, unsteadily, but braced
one against the other,
and commence to pray.

Communion

The river tells my life as it laps,
licks slick clay, twists into its meanders
all the methodologies, the mores,
the strictures of my father.

I splash with the urgency of
my delivery from my mother's womb,
scrabble through drought-barren windings
where struggling fish flop and heave.

In its spates and torrents, the river
swallows up this sacrament of folly:
washed by flood-drunk water onto
overflowing banks, I become an
offering, a host, a Christ-unleavened,
on the river's sand-roughened tongue.

Bellflower

When I read the word *bellflowers*,
the soul of an old monk
pulls the cord that sounds
the carillon of you in my brain:
bright notes of bluebells,
tinkle of mauve-spotted
campanulas, the deep resonance
of peach-glow foxglove.

I see you, bent or on one knee,
hand cupped around corolla:
the momentary but ever
recurring spring that tolls
the completion of each
of my Kansas winters.

Capture

I have captured the butterfly flit of your heart here between my palms. I am ready to open the perfect-bound beating book of you. I feel you explore the boundaries of my whorled skin, my lifeline creases. Your caresses arc from diastolic to systolic. I am ready to receive you with a waft of inhalation, have you measure, with each stretching beat, the volume of my affection. Come, sum milliliters, microns, expand from the appressed space between my clasped hands to the universe surrounding my galaxies of molecules. Plumb my mitochondrial depths. Seek out how my soul intertwines around each of my cells and takes up residence there. I look up at the wide world surrounding us and know the mirrored inverse of that world is here within me. I offer you these poor metrics, these empty estimates, these inadequate assessments of the unbounded quantification of my love.

Alzheimer's

Horrid beast this loss:
memory's index long gone,

stories that made us strong
and independent wrongly

stripped away and, hey,
why are these connections

flipped, as if we'd sipped
too much alcohol, and all

the doors in all the halls
have no numbers; they

confuse us, con us with
cacophony. We cannot

name the flickering faces; they
won't click back into their places.

We have longed to articulate prairies—

to say their names and name
what made them aches in the diaries
of childhoods spent under blue arenas of sky.
Surprise seemed distant as horizons
of featureless crops stretched taut
against Earth's slight undulations.
We grasped their true nature only in views close enough
to see seed heads waving like fingers extended
from steering wheel grips in gritty gravel road passings
beneath a chrome plated sun.

Speak of dust pluming out from a spot on the horizon
that billowed into those we loved on their way home.
Say the way flatness became the metaphor for eternity.
Expostulate on expanses that absorbed what we meant
but never echoed back anything at all expected.
Announce the direction you chose to walk out of all
the infinite choices, all the fractions of degrees opened
by the mathematics of least common denominators.

Tell how the prairies demanded plain language—
diction and drawl and slow twang of distilled meaning
punctuated with silences appropriately scaled
to this exponential burgeoning of land and sky.

Say it, then; say it all.
Say *prairies*.

Relocation

"I have been studying the migration / of the years..."
—Doug Ramspeck, from his poem, "Winter Trance"

The wind, it seems, does not affect the passage of time, the accounts of housewives, keening mad in prairie dugouts, notwithstanding. The stop-time animation of years and seasons that flicker on the inner screen of my eyelids in the intervals between bouts of sleep are never accompanied by a soundtrack of winds. No howls. No shriek of air rushing around the stepped corners of clapboard-sided houses. No murmur of clouds being herded past. Migratory the years may be, but they drift only one way: out, always southing silently, as if the words I fling at you and you at me are being decelerated by the unbelievably viscous flow of time. This traveling, this relocation through the long seasons of life proceeds apace; I feel rather than hear its wake: the parting of air leaves a hollow surrounding my heart that only the inrush of each succeeding breath can measure.

Planting

We have dug in this dirt,
fingers probing into dark loam,
felt the skeins of rootlets,
the squirming grubs,
the pebbles and sand and
organic shreds of long-dead
leaf and petal and stem. We
have felt for moisture's end,
the depth to which our spare
precipitation penetrates, then
dug farther, down to where
the sand or clay underlies it all,
added peat or bone meal,
composted leaves, sloshed
water into the hole, set
a dormant plant's unbound
root ball into this cradle,
this earthy womb, this place
where a thing must be partly
buried to come back to life,
then shoved and tamped
loose earth back into
and around our handiwork,
settled back on our heels,
sighed, listened, and, I swear,
heard the infinitesimal stirrings
of pale root hairs beginning
their search.

A Woodworker's Words - for Pat

I would whittle you a poem,
begin with a green branch
of willow, peel back
the smooth bark and
let you feel the slick,
living phloem, the artery
of the tree, let you imagine
how it ebbs and flows
in some rhythm,
ancient and beyond
our ability to sense,
simultaneously slow as
the seasons and sudden
as the turn from the sleeping
silver of winter to
the quickening green-
gold of March.

I would waft fragrant dunes
of sawdust poems toward you—
the resinous fluff of pine,
the toasty fragments of oak
plucked by steel teeth
spinning and singing
as they worked, the balsam
freshness of cedar, blood-
stained redwood, the dark

and fine-as-talc dust
of teak, the powdery
remnants of boards cross-
cut, ripped, planed to silky

smoothness, of trees gone
to beams and planks,
to flooring and furniture,
to the windows and doors
that open onto the world,
every day, for you.

I would stain you a poem
on marble-smooth
birds-eye maple, the rings
and whorls of years past,
of branches stout as centuries,
lines thinning
and widening, doing
the dance of a tree's
arc of time, splaying,
spiraling, delineating
in Nature's original script
what it would take me
a hundred-life's-worth and more
of my breath to tell you.

3

graphemes & grizzle

grapheme—a letter of an alphabet.
grizzle—bleat; caterwaul; yammer

In Search of a Word

Sonnenizio after a line from Mark Jarman's "Unholy Sonnet"

In their sheer numbers, motes of dust ride, clinging—
motile on the breaths of long-dead bards:
like letters, *mots*, phrase-fragments, words like shards
from books, or notes from a motet—singing,

soaring. You'd swear they are a living motif—
their motive to course shafts of sunlight,
to calm emotions, settle, alight
on books from which voices emote a sheaf

of language—words of pedestrian, motorist,
politician, poet—motivate
us to eliminate rote. Motivate
us to open tomes—to find the *mot juste*—list

the word specific, exact, out of all those motes—
the one motion-captured speck perfection wrote.

Writer's block

is a beggary of words,
        a penury of language,
a mendicancy of compendia,
        dictionaries, glossaries,

lexicons; it measures
        miles on a side, possesses
the density of lead, depleted
        uranium, heavy water, of a million

millstones, contains gluts of
        inaccessible words weighted
down by the infinite gravity
        of the galaxies' blackest holes,

cannot be budged.
        It shades pages, does not
allow letters to seed
        themselves into syllables,

won't allow them to lift
        their leafy swards as words,
to branch into phrases,
        arch over the street as lines,

as stanzas, as poems, chains
        them down, ballasts them,
pins them with hand-forged
        square nails to oak, to ironwood,

to salt-water-hardened
        driftwood, anchors them
in the deepest doldrum depths
        of the Marianas Trench.

Rhyme

You have heard every
rhyme in my repertoire,
can always predict
my next metaphor
and time after time
you say it's a crime
I've never explored
in slant or straight rhyme
what the hell an iamb
is for.

We Citizens

Choose any nine gene fragments
from ten thousand of us; pick
us out for our similarities,
our differences, our shades,
our hues, our height, our stout hearts
our weaknesses, our pronoun
preferences, the width, the breadth
of our facial features; decipher
our molecular phylogenetic
intricacies, wind and wend your way
along the mitochondrial, the nuclear,
include or exclude ribosomal regions,
spring and twine the Fibonacci skeleton
of our DNA, sniff along the ropewalk
spins, the spiral galaxies hidden
in our inner-most and microscopic selves;
mix us, match us, blend us into
what we always have been
in our individuality, our sameness—
children a million times removed
from our ancient and barely
detectable common ancestor—
then try to tell us, your eyes
downcast or piercingly direct,
that we are not, in all our variability,
the same creature.

A paper clip

caresses itself in rounded
        lengths, lies, a flattened spiral,
on the desk, galactic dreams

crushed into practicality. Absent
        opposable digits it yet achieves
grasping, clasping ends,

keeps order amongst unruly
        pages, stains with rust
a theme paper from eight years ago,

impresses embossed images
        of itself onto business letters,
points the same direction

with each of its ends, turns
        180 degrees three times:
thrice, the same number

of times Peter denied Christ,
        his attestations
to the contrary taken as

dictation, scribed in Aramaic
        characters, notarized on sheets
that today would be held together

by this geometry, this form,
        this logical construct,
wrought of wound wire.

Opening the Hall Closet in February

"but westward / ... I sense / the centerfield of summer"
—Ron Wallace, from his poem, "Believing in Leather"

Summer mitt, saddle soap,
cicada chorus, grass-stain
smudges, baseballs hard-edged
as hickory nuts on the bone-
dry winter shelf, rubber-band
bound cards, sweat-banded cap,
dusty visor, and, burning bright
way back, nearly out of sight
in the corner, the tiger-striped
grain of a Louisville slugger.

With Apologies to W. B. Yeats

Your hazel eyes are wind
that stokes the fire in my head,
blows the coals aflame for you,
glimmering girl. Your eyes that
never settle for one hue
or shade, that glint green across
the hilly lands, make of me
a resident of hollow lands
unless I can walk with you
among long dappled grass,
in the emerald gleam of your
glistening eyes, lit by dapples
of the moon, aglow with
dapples of the sun.

Love's Premise

Sanguine sunrise, red wine
surprise, singly starts the day

with promise, the premise being
that dawn sets the direction,

rectifies the tongue's diction,
eliminates lovers' friction,

dereliction of duty forgotten,
less scansion, more music,

we make progress, flex
muscles, take a proud stance,

let acetylcholine prime
memory—mine lexicons

with less choler at noon,
less dissatisfaction at dusk.

Fables for Children of the North

Water Nymph

Wreathe with ferns
your brow, child,
before you wash your hair,

for Rusalka sings
from larch boughs
to entice you to her lair.

Toll Collector

Avoid the shade beneath
the bridge; seek daylight
as you come home,

for trolls in shadow
can bewitch, but
trolls in sun are stone.

Bone Cruncher

Stay hidden in
the timbered depths
of Beowulf's retreat

when Grendel stalks,
through halls of night,
those of us who sleep.

Lies – A Performance Piece for Poet and Chorus

Verse & Chorus 1:   Lies, lies, lies,
No vestige of truth
Betrayals of age,
Inconstancy of youth

We live in a time of artifice over real
The painted-on faces who cheat, lie, and steal

Verse and Chorus 2:   False news, false news
The bald-faced lies
Hints of derision
Fake tears, sham sighs

This factitious, fatuous, illusory world
Genuine given over, the faux news unfurled

Verse and Chorus 3:   Lies, lies, lies,
No vestige of truth
They're actors on stage,
Sly of eye, long of tooth

Talking heads, politicians, experts of disguise
In this age of the global dominion of lies.

Note on rhetorical style for "Lies":
Verses to be read like hard rock/heavy
metal; choruses in style reminiscent of
baroque string accompaniment.

Eschatology

In that last second,
will our senses
become inexplicably
fecund? Will they
flicker, hum
their dirge to ten-
thousand lost tastes,
beckon back
the requisite firsts,
urge the recall
of all those exquisite
bursts? As when,
with dash, élan,
exuberant elation,
eggs, milk, and sugar
become flan—
transubstantiation!

Dear Bookshelf

Libraries and bookstores and dark
dusty Victorian studies with walls
between oak shelving papered
in water-stained velvet share
the million stories that stirred the
neurons of generations of ancestors,
the stories that escaped from the dark
interiors of eggshell skulls as language:
Urdu, Babylonian, Farsi, that passed
from one Mediterranean bard
to another, into the scalloped seashell
ears and out the moist, warm caverns
of tongues and teeth, to arrive, finally,
on cave wall or papyrus scroll,
on the parchment skin of sheep,
to wend their convoluted way
onto paper, strange glyphs of ink
on digested wood, bound up into tomes
and stacked on board shelves, wood
in one form resting on wood in another,
the processions of letters and words
and ideas and tales marching, line
by measured line, page by page,
volume by volume, shelf by shelf,
the route tracing back to the earliest
stories, the ones we have all heard
before, the ones that read
as if they were our own.

Bang

"He grows in the romance / of velocity and range…"
—Harley Elliott

The perverted romance
of the poetry of ballistics
lies in the metaphor of trajectory,
the urgent tug of gravity,
the ballooning cloud
from the nearly instant oxidation
of compounds of carbon,
the supersonic distortion
and splatter of leaden slug
tunneling through meat
and bone, the ratchet and clang
of hollow brass cylinders against
schoolroom halls, locker doors,
office desks, the rising level
of flood borne bile that
always requites nothing.

Euclid and Christ

"I came close once in the triangular / logic of Christ to a mastery"—Stephen Johnson

Christ as the acute apex
of that triangle, base
the opposed Father
and Holy Spirit,
one would suppose,
and perhaps the leg
of the triangle from Father
to Son a right angle, right?
Because Son should be
the shorter distance
from Father although H.S.
did make the *Annunciazione* reality,
so, let's alter that, both legs equal,
angles equal as well, of course,
one leg dipping left, one dipping
right, the Right one for Father,
Conservative, the Left for the Spirit,
the Progressive Aspect
of the Trinity, then, and the Son
the Moderate, neither left
nor right, but centered, in Balance,
Right where the Three of Them
might prefer us to be.

Apologia for Adam

Did God use blueprints?
Adam, all knuckles, knees, elbows,
those complicated shoulder joints—the unkempt
appearance of the first man. Did He begin by collecting
exemplars of other beings? Did every room in His house
fill to overflowing with dozing
zoological specimens all that long, dark first winter?

A golden shovel poem after Donald Hall's "Apology for Old Clothes"

Archipelago

"We live on a little island of the articulate, which we tend to
mistake for reality itself."—Marilynne Robinson

No poem is an island alone;
all poems are archipelagos,
chains of articulation and
interpretation and experience;
and no poem is strictly a narrative
but each poem is a thousand images,
a slide show, a sideshow extravaganza;

no poem is alive until a reader hammers
its chest, puts all her weight into
compressions, all her extra breath
into kisses of life, until she returns
it to sinuous rhythms, to deep
inhalations and measured exhalations,
until the poem stirs, gasping on the sand,
until it rises shakily to its feet, until
it shakes off any pretense and runs
along a shore, reader following,
gesturing, pointing, sometimes
rapturous with laughter, other times
streaming tears of grief salty as the sea,
her bare feet slapping the rhythms of her life
onto the packed wet sands of reality.

4

our extended body

"There is No Environment: The Earth
is Our Extended Body"—Dr. Barry Taylor

Dysfunctional

His harvest: a bumper crop of heartaches;
aspirations tilled under, row after
dusty row; no children's warming laughter;
rusted tractor, dull plow, broken-tined rake;

wife and helpmate's love withered by this drought;
his dry-face grim, gray as the leaning barn;
weed-tangled thoughts that missed signs that warned,
omens that marked him: failed, feckless lout

of a farmer, yokel, oaf, debtor, clod,
broken-axled, flat-tired, fractured man,
ground down so far that he no longer can
attempt to endure, to carry on. "God

help me," he mumbles into a deaf wind,
steps off the hay loft; sows his final sin.

Afire

Fall in September, in ten days. That's soon
enough, except, the month's August-like beginning
(Do you remember? Summer was winning.)
was clearly spelled out in ominous runes:

Triple-digit-temps, grass dry as tinder,
brown the dominant color, yellow ochre.
The dreaded open car window, a smoker,
or a lightning strike: the ridge a lit cinder,

wind sweeping orange flame toward our home.
Prayers and moans, sobs, curses—one or all worked.
The fire turned back up-slope, its momentum burst.
We dropped to our knees: Thank you God. Peace. *Shalom.*

Fall in September. In ten days, perhaps, rain.
The countdown to Autumn begins once again.

The first line is taken from "Eight Days in August: 5" by Marilyn Hacker.

Buzz

A fly bounces against the window like popcorn popping and butter sizzling all at once, his eyes so much of his small self that he knows the path to light is there before him and open to flight, and so his wings row and his halteres stutter and strum and the air hums with the wasted effort of evolution's failure to foresee the transparency of sand become glass.

East, West

The West from left to right,
the East from right to left,
sodden fields awash in rice,
wheat fields: bone dry, bereft.

We'll pit our alphabet against
their logographs that stride—
20,000 strong, unfenced—
leave us confused, wall-eyed.

Preferring our little twenty-six
Roman letters, Latinate,
so easy to match and mix,
literacy's our fate.

Virgil, Ovid, Cicero,
Cui Hao, Wang Wei, Li Po.

Below

My mother's cradle place
was underlain, laced,
by tunnels hacked through coal
by husbands and fathers and brothers,
the place's dark soul known
only by those men, or, at most,
at another remove, by their women,
who woke to the heaving kick
of miner's nightmares: the tremors
born of having seen slabs of slate crush,
the sickening flash of ignited gas burn,
of having dealt with death and worse—
widows, orphans, the wailing ambulance,
the silent hearse.

Exclaiming

Because of the prairie's
plainness, so many things
become exclamation points.

The open-mouthed moon
shouting above the horizon;
the things we deem precious
lifted to the sky: water tower
defying horizontality, church
steeple holding faith in ascendance;
twisting skeins of clouds;
the hulking bulk of grain elevators;
the bright branches of lightning trees.

The single black angus a half-mile
distant—beauty mark on the green
forehead of a Flint-Hills slope.

Legacy

While we debate, delay, conflate, flay science,
heat the atmosphere with the antagonism
of our arrogance, flog logic with the Philistine
phlogiston of corporate greed, set loose to churn
and roil the rhetoric of refused responsibility,

the Earth simmers, the sky smolders
toward spontaneous combustibility,
the spark of conflagration conscripts
the oxygen our grandchildren will gasp for
in the long night of the climate we changed
for them.

Millennia Insecta

I have known the eons-long longing of insects gone to stone:
empty wishes of disjointed plates no longer
encasing throbbing thorax, fecund abdomen; the
craving of coxae that once cupped flexing femurs;

the weariness of wings become limestone lithographs;
the layered years hardened against weather: sturdy slate,
kiln-baked mudstone and siltstone that hold the compressed
millennia of wisps of beings that whisked air under

the sun mere days, then died. And I have seen a day pass
from horizon to horizon in the instant I looked up
from stone to sky, the split second I became aware
of buzzing and flapping, flicking wings, whirring flags

of chitin and scales—all the stalking, searching, pulsating
life arisen from these very foundations of their world.

Nighthawks at Dusk

for Eric Clapton

Nighthawks neglect
the night's knock
knock knocking,
darkness nigh
or not, they soar,
wheel, agitate
purple dusk
with their wing's
striking strip
of white, stir
their piercing calls
into the mix, echo
one another's sweeps
against the sky's swale,
dare the stars to swarm
through heaven's
darkening door.

Revolving Toward that End

"...I laugh / and cry for every turn of the world."
—William Stafford, from his poem, "Why I Am Happy"

The moon, showing its round nature only between parenthetic extremes, helps me interpret the world's ways: the constant mechanics of Newtonian gravity; the revelatory evolution of relativity; the mores of planetary systems of dance; the earth's reason for turning her smitten cheeks; how constellations code the DNA of interstellar black matter; why surface tension makes spheres of my salt-riven tears; how stars invert their patterns onto the curved screen of my optic nerves; why I don this crescent smile to greet the newly-risen sun.

Algorithm

"The smell of fresh growth / ignited the illusion of eternity."
—Pat Beckemeyer

Regrowth and renewal—a sort
of eternity—the only kind we
DNA-driven creatures could
know, some germ of an idea
made manifest as matter, built
by codes and decoders and spirals
of proteins glomming on to one
another. They would click into place
if they weren't so plush with liquid,
so blood- or sap-saturated, but they
do the semi-solid next best thing,
mush together and cling, stretch,
sproing like shock absorbers, cluster
in groups with similar intent, build
another version of what has passed,
another version of what left behind
these blueprints, these plans, these
algorithms of infinitesimal but infinite
plenitude.

Dragonfly

You are the rustling
of cattail leaves, amplified.
You multiply sounds as if
they were the Bible's loaves
and fishes, feed my ears
with the promise of brushings
and stirrings, wings whisking,
whirring, clicking
as you make your way
through phalanx reeds.

Your eyes shutter
sun-shade-sun-shade
variations as you
dart-pause-dart,
as you fix the latitude,
longitude of Sol-dappled prey
onto the globes of your vision.

Bound by water below
and skylight above, you
navigate all that lies between
with pinion-winged-aplomb.

Your wings become translucent
bronze, turn diamond-dazzled clear,
eat up or spit out sparkles of sunlight
flash-chew air, parry: epees, broadswords,
knife-edged-parters of atmosphere
propelling you, rustler of sunlit sounds,
emperor of summer skies.

Soybean Fields

"In farmers' wordlessness / hides the truth…"
—Lori Brack, from her poem "If they don't tell us"

Floods both render
and rend bottomlands,
declare us to be
mere sharecroppers,
decide their share
without consultation,
leave us a few acres,
a consolation prize of sorts,
sort out the real
farmers among us
from the dilettantes.

We may reveal
the depth of our despair
in the dilation of our pupils,
but none will hear
a fret from us about
Cruel Fate, What's Fair.

Shrugs, slumped shoulders,
thumbs hooked around
straps of overalls,
DeKalb caps pulled
low over eyes downcast
at harvest time—tell
the wordless tale quite well—
our farm country pantomime.

Winter Moon

"…the moon and frost bickering over who's prettier." —Li Shangyin

Frost captures every ray
of moon's radiance, traps
both waves and particles
of light in miniscule crystal
palaces where they dance minuets,
sing calls to prayer from minarets,
flicker minimalist messages
of luminance, mime glimmers
of Minke whales in Arctic waters,

whereas

the Moon glazes the whole
world in white haze,
celebrates the February chill
of its splendorous circularity
by rising as if there was
no other reason
for this winter sky.

Stafford County, Kansas

On this salt marsh day
a sheet of barely rippling water,
stilled by November's immensity
of sky, stops just this side of the horizon,
crinks marginal cattails at their waterline,
imprisons in its surface tension the dark
affectations of coots, the shudder
of tuxedoed avocets, the molten flare
of a singular yellow-headed blackbird.

Then this—tarnished sheen of gray sky
sparked with charged particles of plovers—
plovers pluming out and up and around
all at once, tying the air in hairbows, in
delirious knots of birds, then plummeting
earthward, ribboning toward the intimate
confluence of water and air, each racing
neck and neck toward a photo finish
with its own Chang and Eng reflection.

Wheat whisks the wind

with its wiry awns,
takes off the edge,
and thus keeps hold
of dirt and moisture,
pulls sunlight down
and water up
in the ancient alchemy
of gilding the landscape,
making of it
an iconography,
a holy image that blesses
this cathedral: Kansas
at harvest time.

Words for Snow

The white bears have already forgotten the continent of ice;
they think they have dwelt forever on this archipelago of small
and scattered islands.

—The Yupik, indigenous Arctic people traditionally residing in
Siberia, Saint Lawrence Island and the Diomede Islands

Each of the many Yupik words for snow will be written on a sliver
of willow bark, placed in a seal-bladder sac. Year after year words
will be pulled out, one by one, gummed by a toothless elder.
Blubber-oil lights will flicker on their faces as they tell the words.
This is how the people will remember, once the snow has gone:
they will recall blizzards when they see the white cataracts cloud in
an old woman's eyes; when an old man says the word *qetrar*, the
children will repeat it as he describes the feel of the crust of snow
crunching and yielding to the cushion beneath. This is how the
people will remember when white is known only as the color of
clouds, when the land is only mud and stone, when the Arctic Sea
remains lapis-blue the entire winter long.

5

chuchotements

chuchotements - whispers

Photos Missing from an Album

All those moments we didn't save to savor,
times when we failed to say, "Everyone gather,"
take up camera and record the flavor
of what we each felt, some content, others sadder,

a proud face, a clouded visage, an image to jog
our minds, one we might compare, take up in hand
and find, from one or the other, we'd cut the fog
of time, we'd found the point, the exact grain of sand

when one of us found love or lost it or gave
our hearts and souls for one of our children's smiles
or had felt, in hand on shoulder, a wish to save
one of us from pain, to lend strength for a while

to another, to cherish, to offer amnesty,
to do what we do, as members of a family.

Cadenza

You can strum my poem,
pluck at the *em* sounds,
hum its risings and fallings,
its wanderings through
the shapes your mouth
must form for each phoneme.

Use your pen as a mallet
to make percussive use
of punctuation.

Here is another suggestion:
turn the poem sidewise
and imagine each line
is a white or black
key. Now improvise
a new set of chords,
play this poem,
pull out of it
that symphony
you knew I was
conducting when
I wrote it, my fingers
lifting and dropping
from my own keyboard,
hearing each word resonate
with the next in the legato
phrasing I knew
you always loved best.

Sandhill Cranes

cross the night's heavens: shadows
singing pilgrim tales of Aransas,

of Quivira. Chaucer would have
approved, I think, of the lilt, the lift,

the links their calls weave, bird
to bird, birds to earth-bound souls.

In my next life I would be such
a traveler, wading knee-deep

in the Platte, strutting and dancing
on treeless tundra, whipping miles

out of November skies, diving
and laughing beneath Orion's

arching path, winging my way
to the shrines of cranes.

Heart heaving against binding ribs,
furcula springing, I would traverse those

flyways that stretch, like strands
of ancient DNA, across the meandering sky.

You, Lifting

You are always lifting your eyes
 skyward, whether at stars
or clouds, skyscrapers in the night
or an oriole blistering orange
onto the darkening green
of an elm. You always suspend
the mundane for the high instant
that rises and pulls your sight upward,
the Monarch on its busy way to Mexico,
a tamer orange, but fluttering
in a way that your lashes imitate
when you blink away the moisture
the bright sky always brings
to your meridian-seeking eyes.

Summer Walk

The Moiré patterns
of chain-link fences seen
one through another
shimmer ebony waves
onto a sea of green lawns.

The prows of houses
armada into view,
a neighborhood fleet
advancing along
the windswept street.

Alone

"… The wolf knows loneliness the same as / an old woman"
—Melvin Litton, from his poem, "Old Lives"

The loneliness of a solitary predator
is unlike that of pack animals,
is a loneliness of self-imposition,
of anchorite, of penitent, or perhaps
the loneliness of a being who does not need
the comfort of anything organic, needs only
wind ruffling feathers or hair, rain and snow
settling onto back or face, the granite
beneath paw solid as solitude, the branch
entwined by claw rough as the hermit's
unused vocal cords; it is loneliness to be aged
like burgundy, stored in an oak cask, dipped
from bung hole, sipped from ladle, the
tannin and heart's blood fermented,
astringent as its solitary soul.

Surface Tension

Rivers and creeks and lakes and ponds have all learned one magic trick—they paint themselves with sky and pull down onto themselves images of everything that attempts to loom above their flat and self-seeking selves, grasp those pictures, fracture them with every small shimmer, every wavelet, every radiating ring of surface tension disturbed by leaf fall or raindrop, become the carnival hall of mirrors that show the world how fragile even mountains can be when brought to water's level.

Absolution

"... priest holding so many guilty tongues"
—Don Stinson, *"Mors Praematura"*

Forgive me, Father, for
I have sinned again,
and again, and against
so much evidence you
might think I am less
than straightforward,
more transgressor
than confessor; agoraphobic,
perhaps, longing for this safe
haven, this confessional closet,
closeted with my sins
and all the forgiveness
I can never deserve,
all the forgiveness held
in reserve and rolled out,
doled out to me in dollops
of admonitions to sin
no more.

Dormancy

"Believe in dormant buds."—Ken Hada, "February Blues"

"Dormant, not dead,"
becomes our February prayer,
our March mantra. The same
April that brings burgeoning
buds can bludgeon them,
pierce their swollen souls
with icy tendrils.

"Dormant, not dead," we shout,
joining Spring's singing birds,
Lent's lyricists, Easter's chorists
of sacrifice and love.

"Dormant, not dead," we whisper,
Wisteria wafting its sweet, fragrant
reply.

elegy for our father

what we had left was nothing
of him   nothing of his loping
slender grace on the court   nothing
of the casual reach overhead
outfielder's mitt beckoning ball
nothing of the confident hand
on the shoulder of child   of co-worker
the unruly boy   the quiet husband
the 43-year old paled by pain
the laborer   the township clerk
the fisherman   the grower of potato
beet green-bean   of cabbage corn radish
nothing of any of that   nothing
of what it was we saw on the red
screen of our closed eyes
nothing our tears could conjure
nothing of his hand pointing out
pole star   his hand arching a plum
in orbit around an orange   his finger
running down a dictionary page   nothing
of his finger pointing to each letter of a word
his lips forming phonetic bits
nothing of his arms enfolding our mother
all that is not left   all that we knew
him by   all that we thought ourselves
to be   nothing of that   nothing of him
but what he placed there each moment
each day of our lives   in our hearts
hands heads   nothing of him   but us but
us   but us

Forests

The deeper the shade of green the stronger
the attraction—the way green shadows
toward blue, the way light is sent away
scowling at having to yield dominance,
the way the optic nerves relax, the green
flow of neuron mantras soothing
inflamed pathways; the way green
grows from seedling to canopy, coiling
and twining, the infinitude of leaf green,
the cool depths and drifts of what was
once green resting beneath the still
and quiet of what has become
the deepest and truest shade of it.

Rainstorm Reminiscence

The rain in Kansas, seldom seen
ghost of itself in those better days
of memory, is but a transient whiff
of clean-scented air, of dust brought
to ground, a peripheral glimpse
of a glint of sunlight caught
in a droplet of water at the tip
of a remembered leaf, the merest
eye-blur hint of spectral colors arching
across a sky of billows, is a spirit
recollection floating across a field,
a pale sheaf of water streaming
from gray heaven to parched pasture,
the moist rhythm of drops strumming
leaf, stem, a childhood lullaby
dimly recalled whispering
against the white noise
of silence.

One Step at a Time

You try to smooth my rough edges,
hammer at the bumps, planish
me, until the light catches
you, mirrored, and you wish
me into this perfect reflection
of your own sought-for perfection.

Hospice

My heart's two
halves: a pair of old
muddy boots;

enough sole,
I suppose, to
trudge a few

more pebbled paths
of days, more
leathery gray hours.

I eke out
translations
into the braille

of uneven breath,
rip-edged rasp
of intake, out-heave,

repetitious pledge,
gain a grip on a
pedestrian truth:

the implausible
deniability
of the end of this life.

Myth of Innocence

Follow my lead
Navigate the shoals
Do not fly too close to the sun
All her mother's
       cautions
The soothing shadow of wings
Pinioned to her side
Daughters can only be protected for a little
       time
While the white heat of men's sons radiates
Reflects off
       all the surfaces of the world
Lights up clouds   Attracts daughters
      Fevers them   Unfetters their defenses
Too close   the softening of determination
      The bees' wax of waning aloofness
Fluttering   Scattering of down
      Quills and pinions
Heat of the moment
      Falling
The sudden cooling oceanic plunge back into resolve

Names

Forty days
and nights

of rain say
the names

of all man's
children and

of all God's
animals, calls

the roll of
the non-extinct

bobbing on waters
roiling, peering

through the forest
of rain's stalks

of falling, feeling
the tattoo

onto ear drums
the constant tap

of code that appends
the honorific *Saved*

to each creature's
Holy Name.

Sonnenizio on a Line from Berryman's Sonnet 25

Irresponsible, since all the stars rain blind
tonight, obscured by clouds that allay their light
and you might allege, darkness of the sane mind—
allegorical stories of philosophers, out of sight

stage left or right; they rap allegro tunes to us
shift to an allemande, invite us to dance,
but never do they alleviate concern; we still fuss
with allegations: suspicion, sidewise glances.

Rain or tears let's make our alliance tight.
Here, rhyme and alliteration will abound:
whether short or tall, whether wrong or right,
we'll allocate words to each surging sound;

then allot, since tonight's stars only rain blind,
unalloyed luminescence of another kind.

6

mouth brimming over

"heart and mouth brimming over"—Oscar Levy

Allegory

We are continents adrift. This rift between us bears
the shape of all we shared—watery space that's bound
by paths we traced round obstacles, the trackless sea
of uncertainty chronicled in logbooks of memory:

averted glances, furtive looks, the muttered apologies
we longed to say, the mythology of siren songs, the ruddered-
turns to face away, shuttered hatches, safe havens shoaled.
The once phosphorescent waves, now old, waft the scent—

the seaweed spume of love lost. Looming storms have tossed
us each onto opposing shores—breached by tsunami roars
of consternation: the roving, transient tectonic plates—
the ship-wreck navigation of uncaring fates, the map's

jagged outlines—the way their jigsaw fit aligns, the jaw-
clenched words you find and spit: *The Hell with it.*

Blackberry

Orbed agglutinant
of midnight regality:

purple, globular. Balloon-
burst of seeds, bright-juiced

pips. Oberon's choice for fairy
feasts. Burgundy molecule,

orbit of syrups, black nectars
bound in roundness. Mouth-

mesmerizing mounds. Drencher
of tongue, palate, tonsil.

Temptress piercer of fingertips.
Giver-up of galaxies, of black holes

that dwell between the luscious confines
of cheeks and lips. Most liquid

of labials. Once eaten, imbibed,
you make me feel immoral,

immortal. Make of me your
enamored berry inamorato!

Connoisseurs of Verse

> "Seventh grade, the boy is set to memorizing one
> of Shakespeare's sonnets, and he reads it and rereads it
> —it becomes his cud—" —Albert Goldbarth

Mark Strand devoured it. Albert's boy masticates it, regurgitates it, ungulate style, with burly bovine intent. We could try pantoum fricassee, bury an ode in hot coals like a south seas hog, make a luau of it, pick metaphors from between our teeth, wash it all down with Whitman's ale, Wordsworth's plonk. Sear the sweetbreads of Plath, sample the bento box of haiku, toss the empty peanut shells onto Ginsberg's floor. Let's chew on the taut words of performance poets, like dogs with their rawhide bones, our eyes glazed over, our canines scratching at each stanza, scraping off syllables small enough to swallow, tearing off a line that seems to grow as we chomp, tough and rubbery as calamari, dense with unexpressed regret, sinewy as unsuppressed rage.

Late Summer Haibun

Our neighborhood settles back on grizzled haunches: houses with shuttered eyes, lawns lazed over with August haze. Adults have been led by the hand by briefcases and toolboxes to Accuras and F150's. Kids voice cadenza daydreams of lost summer against teachers' chorus of welcomes. My dog is deeply invested in sauna sidewalks and squirming reveries; I drip sweat as humid air condenses on my lemonade: tall glass still life, visual mantra. A convict-striped bumblebee rumbles up to the flower bed, shuffles into a bellflower, backs out dazed by a flash-bang explosion of fluorescent yellow pollen. Together, bee and I watch the ultraviolet sky polarize, feel magnetic declination align the hematite in our bellies with lines of longitude, hear the faint tink and creak of winter waking in the far-off Yukon Territories. September settles her heel into fall's starting block. In all this prescient stillness we listen for what we know is out there, watch for Nature's tells, try to predict the last card she holds, face down, on the green felt of this late summer day.

> oriole eye-jolt,
> brash orange, black glimmer,
> sun's bright acolyte

Neuroses

"... wine and roses, profound neuroses"—Don Stinson

Rose hip wine.
This obsession of mine.
The fermentation of love
into something astringent,
a lamentation, Vincent
at his palette, straining
at the alchemy of making
pigment redefine reality.
Wheat fields run amok,
friends who refuse to truck
in imagery this oblique.
Still life of leek and shallot,
the vase of sunflowers leering
back, peering into a painter's
neurosis, the artist's closest
brush with the absolution
of confession, the blotches
on the canvas he could never
bring himself to mention.

Royalty

should be illegal—the regal use of purple,
the passing down of crown to well-fed, to plump
children born of illustrious loins, silver spoon, plum
thumbed with appropriate heredity, bishop's palm
on babe's head, the christening, the plummet
of holy water onto brow, wet nurse, festive pudding,
well-fed child of royal genes, scent of rosemary, pungent
myrrh, ears filled with purrs, prayers, lullabies plangent,
lines of ancestry in manuscripts, lists of lineages the panacea,
the first and last, the *raison d'être*, of all this empty panache

Sunset

Dragonfly fluttering
in the dust-filtered
evening twilight,
warping
the sun's last lingering,

like a supernova altering
the last gravity of the day,

like a mouth-harp player
bending,
from B to B-flat,
the last note of evensong,

like a cue ball clicking
just off center,
breaking,
breaking,
breaking the racked light.

Vermeer

liked his surfaces flat,
broad, well-defined,
at angles right or
acute, blocks of space
to be washed by light,
light coming at them
through half-opened doors
or windows, through small
facets of hand-blown glass
or stained glass, shaded
by frames separating
light through glass
from light through openness,
all to provide a background
for light lingering on the full
rounded faces, the graceful
curves of cheekbones and
chins, the sweeping bisection
of faces by the bridges of noses,
the foreheads, the caresses
of light dwindling to soft shade,
the mellowness of lit-up lips,
the highlight shine of eyes
windowing what we see now,
what he saw then, what his
subjects see as they look
back at us from light-years
away.

Milking

The hollow lives
of cows, the stainless
steel lips of their metal-
boned calves almost
silently slurping,
the pneumatic tail-slap
of valves, the urgent rush
of milk from gland
to tubing.

Geometria

The analytical geometry of animals:
the ballistic parabolas of frog hops,
the travelling waves of dogs shaking
off water in volute sheets, the top-
spinning nutating ellipses of twirling
whirligig beetles, the sinusoidal scuttering
of snakes on sand, the organized
near-chaos of clouds of birds swelling
and shrinking their three-dimensional
amoebic morphology through a blue
sea of sky, the knot-theorist's challenge
to describe the twining limbs
of animal love.

I am the moon

this eleventh month
day's beginning.

Crescent grin, one
morning star eye. I

mount the eastern dark
in my slow rise, huff frost

onto grass spikes, lave
the lawn with winter's

breath, then drag up
the salmon-leafed

dawn to spark cold
ice with fire.

Family Games

olly-in-free moon
mother goose
spells and runes
shoelaces loose
childhood friends
summer's end
father's ruse
you can't depend on

family games, family games
you said you'd be back
but you never came

snitch a purse
play with matches
school nurse sees
bruises, scratches
rain in gutters
windows shuttered
backyard latches
stammers, stutters

runny nose
pick-up ball
last one chosen
no one to call
grandma's house
muffled shouts
run and fall
fire stomped out

grow up fast
hardscrabble street
bad-times last
nervous feet
deceit and folly
the sky keeps fallin'
delete delete
divorce they call it

family games, family games
you said you'd be back
but you never came

Gavotte

My dog, gallivanting
where her nose leads,
follows a serpentine path
that knots, twines like
the best efforts of Gordius,
while I, no Alexander, cut
straight through the morning.

Who's to say my gadabout
isn't right, that I am too eager
by far to get to the finish line,
to complete each morning, each
week, in a dead gallop toward
the same glib end.

She strolls the grass
in her intricate cursive;
I stride, my steps hard-angled,
bold, sans serif.

She, geomancer, gourmand
of the ground's intricate secrets,
must pity me, blind as I am
to the geode gleam she gleans
from every singular step
of each day's dance.

At Home on the Shore

The homes of mollusks almost never
go on the market, no matter how lovely,
how brilliantly constructed.

Oh, certainly hermit crabs will use
a discarded shell, turn it into their own
private Winnebago, but most
just drift, end up half-buried
on some white sand beach
until, on another storm-drenched
tropical night, a wave dislodges
them wholesale, and at once
there goes the neighborhood,
afloat, adrift, scattered.

Their colors fade, the shiny
surfaces scour, their chalky bones
begin to show, minerals go back
into suspension in the sea
from which they were built.

And somewhere, in some decrepit
tenement of an oyster bed,
a Wellfleet or Kumamoto slushes
seawater through its gills,
haphazardly adds to its shaggy,
craggy shell, and devotes all its art
instead to the pearl it hides within.

Cartography

"They of the trembling hands and liver spots
like a map of Asia, far pale countries of the flesh…"
—B. H. Fairchild, from his poem, "Old Women"

What if our hands took on, in aging's unbidden
tattoos—a charisma of cartograms—liver
spot lineages of all the places, severe
or elegant, we ever visited: middens

of melanin, maps of solar lentigines.
What if our faces became globes, continents afloat
on a wrinkled sea, the places we'd trekked, remote
or nearby, Polynesian isles, the Pyrenees.

We would each be an illustrated chronicle,
walking travel journal, topographic treatise,
destined, not for the grave upon our quietus,
but a Special Collections shelf, as an anatomical

atlas, chart of voyages made, map as yet unfolded,
a plot of a life's treasure sites, waiting to be decoded.

Acknowledgements and Notes:

Thanks, as always, to my wife and fellow poet Pat, the love of my life, my best friend, and my constant inspiration.

The Wayward Poets are still typing and writing away on a nearly weekly basis after almost 10 years of mutual inspiration. Current members are Jane Ray, Judy Hatteberg, Dixie Brown, Melany Pearce, Pat Beckemeyer, Pat Latta, and Carol Neighbors.

The Basement Bards critiqued many of these poems and helped to greatly improve them: Skyler Lovelace, Diane Wahto, Dave Cook, Pat Beckemeyer, and Bob Dean—*Muchas gracias*!

Raylyn Clark and April Pameticky continue to bring new poetic faces together every month at *ICT Poets* at the Advanced Learning Library in Wichita, Kansas for workshops and critiques. Thanks to them both and to all participants who have helped to shape some of the work in this book.

Thanks, as well, to fellow writers of the *Kansas Authors Club* for continued support and encouragement, particularly Kristine Polansky, who first encouraged me to try my hand at classical forms of poetry.

I appreciate the editorial board of Blue Cedar Press for their enthusiastic support and insightful advice; a special thanks to Michael Poage and Gretchen Eick.

Finally, note that some of these poems appeared first elsewhere, sometimes in a different form. Thanks to editors of these venues for choosing to publish my work.

"Allegory"— first appeared in *Bards Against Hunger: Kansas* (Kevin Rabas, 2018, Local Gems Press, Long Island, NY), in a slightly different form. This sonnet eschews end rhymes but incorporates varied internal rhyming. The first 13 lines of the poem vary from 12 to 15 syllables; the last line is in iambic pentameter to provide further emphasis for the *volta* which finally occurs there.

Aransas is a National Wildlife Refuge in Texas where Sandhill and Whooping Cranes overwinter.

"Artifact"—*KYSO Flash*, Summer, 2019.

auricle—the mostly cartilaginous portion of the external ear; an atrium of the heart.

"Below"—was inspired by a line, "…Mama's cradle place"—by Atsuro Riley, from his poem, "Scroll."

"Blackberry"—*KYSO Flash*, Summer, 2019.

"Buzz" —Halteres are the hind wings of true flies (insects in order Diptera) that have been altered to club-like appendages that serve the insect as gyroscopes measuring its orientation in space.

"Cartography"—Solar lentigines are small melanotic spots on the skin caused by sun exposure.

"Cathedral"—*KYSO Flash*, 2019.

"Celebration"—was inspired by the line "…every girl hums her own lithe youth…" by Laura Madeline Wiseman & Andrea Blythe, from their poem, "Every Girl Becomes the Wolf."

"Connoisseurs of Verse"—*KYSO Flash*, Summer, 2019.

"Conch Shells as Conveyances"—*KYSO Flash*, Summer, 2019.

"Dysfunctional"—First appeared as "Dsyfunctional" (purposely misspelled) in *Somewhere Between Kansas City and Denver* (Spartan Press, 2019, Edited by Jason Ryberg). The poem was inspired by Ted Kooser's "Abandoned Farmhouse."

"Declension"—This poem contains the Latin scientific names of poison ivy (*Toxicodendron radicans*) and the American robin (*Turdus migratorius*). It takes its title from the last two lines: "agricola, agricolae, / agricolorum" —a portion of the declension of the Latin noun for farmer or agriculturalist.

"East, West,"—was inspired by a line by A. E. Stallings: "Writing left to right… as a broken beast furrows a field," from her poem, "Art Monster."

"Emigrants, 1857"—Dedicated to the memory of my paternal great-great grandparents, Heinrich and Christiene Beckemeyer, who emigrated with eight of their children from Minden, Prussia, to the United States.

"Fables for Children of the North"—*Silver Birch Press*, October 28, 2014.

fanfaronade—a grandiose trumpet blast.

"Fifty-Eighth Anniversary" is for my wife, Pat; our 58th anniversary was on November 23, 2019.

"Fire and Water" — was inspired by the line: "…nothing / but the language of movement" by Michael Cissell, from his poem "My Friend Is a Fish."

"*Gavotte*" —*KYSO Flash*, 2019.

grapheme—a letter of an alphabet.

grizzle—bleat; caterwaul; yammer.

"At Home on the Shore"—*Mockingheart Review*, 2019.

"Hail, *Amphibia*"—*KYSO Flash*, Summer, 2019.

"Hospice"—*KYSO Flash*, 2018.

"Ikhthýs"—*I-70 Review*, 2019. "Ikhthýs"— "a representation of a fish used … as a Christian symbol for the Greek word ichthys interpreted as an acrostic in which the Greek letters are the initials of the words … meaning Jesus Christ Son of God Savior" (Merriam -Webster Unabridged Dictionary). Now "…known colloquially as … the 'Jesus fish'" (Wikipedia). Inspired by the line, "…the Jesus fish my students and their parents proudly display on their pick-up truck bumpers…" by Michael Cissell, from his poem, "How to Scream a Fish"

"In Search of a Word"—*Somewhere Between Kansas City and Denver* (Spartan Press, 2019, Edited by Jason Ryberg).

"Legacy" —*KYSO Flash*, Summer, 2019.

"Love's Premise"—*I-70 Review*, 2018 Issue.

"*Mephitis mephitis*"—*Gasconade Review*, 2019. The title is the scientific name of the North American striped skunk.

"Nighthawks at Dusk"— *Flint Hills Review*, 2019.

Quivira is a National Wildlife Refuge in Kansas where Sandhill Cranes rest on their migration.

"Rainstorm Reminiscence"—*Flint Hills Review*, 2019.

"Revolving Toward That End" —*KYSO Flash*, 2018.

"Singing to Myself"—*365 Poems: A Poetry Anthology Vol. 2*, 2018. The *kaihōgyō* ("circling the mountain") is an ascetic practice of Buddhist monks that involves walking a route on Mount Hiei while offering prayers at halls, shrines and other sacred places.

sonnenizio—noun—a form invented by Kim Addonizio: "...fourteen lines...start with a line from someone else's sonnet. Repeat one word from that line in every successive line of the poem. The last two lines have to rhyme."—p. 254, *Ordinary Genius*, 2009, W. W. Norton & Co., NY & London.

"Spring Floods" was inspired by the line: "Praise my coronary artery, the Red River," by Jenny Molberg, from her poem, "Invocation."

"Sunset"—*The Syzygy Poetry Journal*, April 4, 2016.

"Surface Tension"—*KYSO Flash*, Summer, 2019.

"Vermeer"—*365 Poems: A Poetry Anthology Vol. 2*, 2018.

"Winter Moon"—*Flint Hills Review*, 2019.

"With Apologies to Walt"— first appeared in the online journal *KYSO Flash* in 2018 in a slightly different form and wording.

"A Woodworker's Words—for Pat"—*Gasconade Review*, 2019.

"Words for Snow"—*KYSO Flash*, 2018; this prose poem was nominated by *KYSO Flash* and selected for publication in *Best Small Fictions*, 2019.

The Author

Roy Beckemeyer and his wife Pat live in Wichita, Kansas. His poems have appeared in more than half a dozen anthologies and a variety of print and on-line journals. His first collection of poetry, *Music I Once Could Dance To* (Coal City Press, 2014) was a Kansas Notable Book. He co-edited, with Kansas Poet Laureate Emerita Caryn Mirriam-Goldberg, *Kansas Time+Place: An Anthology of Heartland Poetry* (Little Balkans Press, 2017). His chapbook of ekphrastic poems inspired by various artists' representations of angels, *Amanuensis Angel*, was published by Spartan Press (2018); his latest poetry book, *Stage Whispers* (Meadowlark Books, 2018) received the Nelson Poetry Book Award in 2019. His work has been nominated for *Pushcart* and *Best of the Net* recognition and was chosen for *Best Small Fictions 2019*. Visit his author's page at https://royjbeckemeyer.com.